COLUMBUS IB H.S.

P9-DHS-233

LOS ANGELES UNIFIED SCHOOL DISTRICT
ISD-86-04-01 FORM # 98.37 (6/86)

ESEA IV-B 197?

741.5 Deur, Lynne

P. it'
t

A Pull Ahead Book

political cartoonists

Lynne Deur

741.5
DEu
11/78   c.2
495

LIBRARY
COLUMBUS JUNIOR HIGH SCHOOL
LOS ANGELES CITY SCHOOLS

Lerner Publications Company • Minneapolis, Minnesota

LOS ANGELES UNIFIED SCHOOL DISTRICT
ESEA TITLE IV-B-S19

ACKNOWLEDGMENTS: The illustrations are reproduced through the courtesy of: pp. 3, 4 (left, right, and bottom), 14, 15, 16, 18, 20, 21, 22, 23, 27, 28, 33, 36, 37, 45, Library of Congress; p. 7, Professional Picture Service; p. 8, © 1962, The Chicago Sun-Times, reproduced by courtesy of Wil-Jo Associates, Inc. and Bill Mauldin; p. 10, Pennsylvania Academy of The Fine Arts; p. 12, The New York Public Library, Astor, Lenox, and Tilden Foundations; p. 19, Culver Pictures, Inc.; p. 29, The New York Public Library; pp. 30, 38, 53, Independent Picture Service; pp. 34, 43, Dictionary of American Portraits, Dover Publications, Inc.; pp. 40, 41, 42, Collection of Ira and Nancy Glackens; pp. 44, 46, Pulitzer Prize Cartoons by Dick Spencer III, The Iowa State College Press; p. 48, John M. Henry; p. 49, 50, 51, Des Moines Register, reproduced by courtesy of John M. Henry; pp. 52, 54, 55, 56, Daniel Fitzpatrick, St. Louis Post-Dispatch; pp. 58, 60, 61, 62, William Gropper; p. 63, Herbert Block; p. 64, Herbert Block, © 1954, The Washington Post Company, "I Have Here In My Hand" from Herblock's Here and Now, Simon and Schuster, 1955; p. 66, reprinted by permission of the Newspaper Enterprise Association, Inc; p. 67, Wide World Photos, Inc.; p. 68, Bill Mauldin; p. 69, © 1963, The Chicago Sun-Times, reproduced by courtesy of Wil-Jo Associates, Inc. and Bill Mauldin; p. 70, drawings © 1944 by United Features Syndicate, Inc., reproduced by courtesy of Bill Mauldin; p. 71, © 1958, St. Louis Post-Dispatch, reproduced by courtesy of Bill Mauldin; p. 72, © 1962, The Chicago Sun-Times, reproduced by courtesy of Wil-Jo Associates, Inc. and Bill Mauldin; p. 73, Bill Sanders; pp. 75, 76, Bill Sanders, The Milwaukee Journal; p. 77, Ray Osrin; pp. 78, 79, Ray Osrin, The Plain Dealer; p. 80, Wayne Stayskal; pp. 81, 82, Wayne Stayskal, Chicago Today; pp. 83, 84, Tom Darcy; p. 85, Tom Darcy, Newsday, Los Angeles Times Syndicate.

LIBRARY OF CONGRESS CATALOGING IN PUBLICATION DATA

Deur, Lynne.
    Political cartoonists.

    (A Pull Ahead Book)
    SUMMARY: A brief discussion of the techniques and functions of political cartoons accompanies capsule biographies of sixteen political cartoonists from Ben Franklin to Tom Darcy.

    1. Cartoonists, American—Juvenile literature.   2. United States—Politics and government—Caricatures and cartoons—Juvenile literature. [1. Cartoonists. 2. United States—Politics and government—Caricatures and cartoons] I. Title.

NC1305.D4   741.5'973   72-128809
ISBN 0-8225-0463-4

Copyright © 1972 by Lerner Publications Company. All rights reserved. International copyright secured. Manufactured in the United States of America. Published simultaneously in Canada by J. M. Dent & Sons Ltd., Don Mills, Ontario.

International Standard Book Number: 0-8225-0463-4
Library of Congress Catalog Card Number: 72-128809

Second Printing 1973

contents

Mr. Dry by Rollin Kirby

Uncle Sam has changed over the many years he has been used in political cartoons. Striped pants and a top hat are the only familiar features of the Uncle Sam pictured in a cartoon from 1840 (bottom). During the Civil War (upper left), Uncle Sam became taller, grew a beard, and in other ways began to look like Abraham Lincoln. By the end of World War I (upper right), he was drawn as a very fatherly, dignified figure.

The Cartoonist's Art

Political cartooning is essentially a symbolic and satiric art. Symbols are a kind of "shorthand" a cartoonist uses to get across his points. Everyone recognizes symbols such as "Uncle Sam" for the United States government, the elephant for the Republican party, or the Statue of Liberty for American freedom and democracy. A cartoonist can use such figures again and again in his drawings without having to label them or worry that his readers may not clearly understand what they mean.

Symbols do change, however, and old ones disappear while new ones appear. Uncle Sam has been used in political cartoons since at least 1832, but throughout the 19th century he didn't look much like today's Uncle Sam. Before World War I "Columbia," a female figure, was used as often as Uncle Sam to symbolize the United States; today she is no longer drawn in political cartoons. In the mid-1940s Herblock created a cartoon figure which he labeled "Mr. Atom." Later, after Mr. Atom had been used in many cartoons, the figure alone was enough to indicate to people what was meant: Mr. Atom became a true symbol.

Symbols are a cartoonist's shorthand, while satire is most often the tool he uses to shape his materials and make his points. Satire makes evil seem not only evil—but foolish and stupid. A drawing of fat vultures with the heads of well-known politicians satirizes the politicians; that is, it makes them look stupid at the same time their greed and ambition is being compared to a vulture's. A picture of a dove (symbol for peace) beating a hawk (symbol for war) over the head with a "Peace" sign satirizes human "doves" who resort to violence in their "fight" for peace. A cartoonist's satire may be funny and playful, or serious and even vicious. (The dove-hawk cartoon is playful; the vulture cartoon more vicious.) But all satire attempts to make its object look foolish. Satire is a very effective weapon because it attacks where people are weakest: no one wants to be seen as a fool or an idiot.

"A Group of Vultures Waiting for the Storm to Blow Over—'Let Us PREY.'"—1871. Thomas Nast satirized the corrupt "Boss" Tweed (front) and his pals, who controlled the government of New York City and grew fat on the people's money.

Political cartoonists, however, although they work with satire and symbols, are not mainly artists or humorists. They are men with ideas and convictions about the events of their own time—and a talent for expressing those ideas and convictions in pictures.

"Couldn't We Negotiate?"—1965. Bill Mauldin makes fun of human beings who strongly oppose warfare but seem willing enough to engage in bloody battles for their cause.

Their pictures are usually satiric but they may be straightforward. They may be mild or they may be forceful. But pictures that are good political cartoons present ideas in such a way that people think about them, remember them, and are moved to do something about them. Political cartoons are like editorials. (In fact, today they are often called editorial cartoons and political cartoonists are called editorial cartoonists.) Editorials express in words the opinions of an individual or group of individuals. Editorials are not objective reports. They attempt to convince the reader to think or feel a certain way about an idea, a person, or a situation or event of current interest. And they attempt to convince by giving reasons or appealing to people's emotions. Political cartoons try to do the same things. And they are as effective and important as editorials, in part because a picture can often make a point that would be difficult or impossible or simply boring to make in writing. Also, they have a larger audience: many people who would not bother to read an editorial are influenced by the cartoons on the editorial pages of a newspaper or magazine.

Benjamin Franklin

(1706-1790)

America's first political cartoonist was not mainly a cartoonist at all. He is usually remembered as an editor, publisher, author, scientist, inventor, politician, and diplomat—nearly everything but a political cartoonist. The man was, of course, Benjamin Franklin. And the crude sketches he used to illustrate ideas in his writings have gone down in history as America's first political cartoons.

Young Ben was an excellent reader and a good student. However, his family was large and unable to handle the expense of education. So after only two years of school, Ben went to work with his father. But Ben did not take to his father's trade of candle and soap maker. Instead, he longed to go to sea. His father disapproved; he wanted Ben to work on land. Finally, when Ben was 12 it was decided: he would serve as an apprentice to his older brother James, a printer.

As publishers and printers of the newspaper called *The New-England Courant*, the Franklins were soon in trouble. Writing under the name of Mrs. Silence Dogood, Ben took his opportunity to poke fun at stern Puritan leaders. The strict, respectable Puritans did not always appreciate the paper's satire. The prominent clergyman Increase Mather was especially upset. He urged the government to "supress such a cursed libel," lest "some awful judgement should rise, and there should be no remedy." James was sent to jail on a petty charge and later ordered to stop printing the paper. In 1723 Ben, who had often been at odds with his brother, left for Philadelphia to open his own print shop.

Young Ben Franklin (with hat) in his brother's printing shop in Philadelphia. Everyone is congratulating him for his first weekly newspaper column, except his jealous brother James (right).

For more than 20 years Franklin's time was devoted mainly to writing, publishing, and printing. With the *Pennsylvania Gazette* and *Poor Richard's Almanack*, he became well known both in the colonies and in Europe. Yet many men and women could not read in Franklin's time.

Symbols or simple pictures were very important. A symbol of Great Britain, a lion or a unicorn, was carved in wood or stone to mark a public building. A thirsty traveler who could not read looked for a sign with a mermaid, the symbol of a tavern. Thus it was not surprising that the gifted young Franklin turned to illustrations to make his points clear.

In 1747 Franklin drew what some historians call his first political cartoon. It appeared in his pamphlet *Plain Truth*. The Pennsylvanians, Franklin warned, needed to unite and defend their colony against the threat of the French and Indians. But the peaceful Quakers were not about to join hands in warfare. To make matters worse, the more militant Christians could see no reason to fight for the pacifists. To show the senselessness of the situation Franklin drew a wagon stuck in mud. The driver knelt in the mud, praying to Hercules. The caption read "Non Votis," or, in effect, "God helps those who help themselves."

Franklin's first political cartoon, "Non Votis"—1747.

Franklin's "Non Votis" was crude and left plenty of room for improvement. Later his drawings were more direct. In 1754 at the Albany Congress Franklin urged the colonies to unite. To illustrate his point he drew a snake divided into eight parts, each representing a colony. (At that time there was a popular superstition that a severed snake would return to life if it were put back together before sunset.)

"Join or Die"—1754.

Franklin fittingly titled his drawing "Join or Die." Within a month the cartoon had been reprinted in every newspaper in the colonies. Later, as the colonies revolted, it became a popular newspaper heading. Franklin used the snake again in a drawing entitled "Don't Tread on Me."

Ben Franklin's career as a political cartoonist was a limited one. Certainly his contributions in other areas were more outstanding. But the professionals since have probably only dreamed of making the impact on their audiences that Franklin did with his simple snake.

Self-portrait of Thomas Nast

Thomas Nast

(1840-1902)

On September 27, 1840, a boy was born in an army barracks in Landau, Germany. His father was a trombone player in the Bavarian army—and a man who was not afraid to express his political views. Six years later the family arrived in New York City. Here the boy, Thomas Nast, would influence the politics of his new country with his artistic talent and strong viewpoints.

Tom Nast was not a good student. Art was his only interest. "Go finish your picture," his teacher once told him. "You will never learn to read or figure." By the age of 15 the young artist had left school and was looking for a job. He found one with *Frank Leslie's Illustrated Newspaper*. Nast's assignments were many and varied; they took him from boxing matches to a war in Italy.

The American Civil War helped bring Thomas Nast to fame. *Harper's Weekly* hired the artist to cover the conflict. Nast stood firmly for the Union cause—so firmly that many declared the Confederates would have burned him at the stake had they captured him. With his drawings Nast stirred his readers' sympathy by showing the Yanks as kind and gentle men in the midst of a bloody war they had never wanted. At the same time he aroused the fury of Northerners by showing the Confederate soldiers as cruel and brutal. President Lincoln spoke of Nast as "the Union's best recruiting sergeant."

"Compromise with the South"—1864.

Nast's fury did not end as the war drew to a close. When appeasers wanted to bring the South back into the Union with as little trouble as possible, Nast drew his famous cartoon "Compromise with the South." The drawing showed "Columbia" (at that time a common symbol of the United States) weeping as she buried the dead. Standing over her with a foot on the grave, a haughty Confederate grasps the hand of a downcast and legless Union soldier. Nast wanted to show that following the appeasers' plans would in effect make the South the victor of the Civil War; he felt that the South should be severely punished.

At the end of the war Thomas Nast, who was then only 25, had the high points of his career ahead of him. He began his own war against "Boss" Tweed and the Tammany Hall politicians in New York City. Tweed and his puppets controlled the city's government and had turned it into their private money-making machine. Courageously, Nast set about to destroy that machine. Again and again his cartoons lashed out at the Tweed Ring.

"Boss" Tweed

"Who Stole the People's Money?—'Twas him.'"-1871.

"Boss" Tweed had established his image as a great, kind, charitable man of wealth. The artist drew Tweed as a fat scoundrel, a thief. Tweed began to fear Nast. Then another Nast cartoon—"Who Stole the People's Money?"— showed Tweed and his associates in a circle, each pointing to the other. "'Twas him," were their answers. Tweed was enraged. "Let's stop them damn pictures," he shouted. "I don't care so much what the papers say about me—my constituents can't read; but damn it, they can see pictures!"

No bribe or threat could stop Nast. Shortly before a city election Nast drew a tiger pawing at a dead body in a huge arena. The caption read "The Tammany Tiger Loose—'What are you going to do about it?'" With this cartoon Thomas Nast won his war. "Boss" Tweed and his friends were ousted from office.

"The Tammany Tiger Loose—'What are you going to do about it?'"—1871.

Nast's "Merry Old Santa Claus"—1884.

The fall of the Tweed Ring made Nast a public figure. But Tweed's collapse was not Nast's only accomplishment. The cartoonist's strong stand for Ulysses S. Grant for President helped put the ex-general into public office. Grant himself declared, "Two things elected me: the sword of Sheridan and the pencil of Nast." Nast also established the elephant as a symbol for the Republican party. On the lighter side, our image of Santa Claus is based on Nast's drawings of the jolly fellow.

Unfortunately for his career, Santa Claus was the only subject Nast drew with good-natured wit. Thomas Nast's courage, integrity, and drive were clouded by his unrelenting bitterness. When Horace Greeley ran for President, Nast's cartoons turned into savage attacks on an old enemy. (Greeley, as publisher of the *New York Tribune*, had been slow to admit that "Boss" Tweed was a thief.) Nast never tired of attacking Greeley. One of his last cartoons in the campaign, "We are on the home stretch," showed Greeley being carried off on a stretcher. It was not humorous. The candidate's wife had just died and Greeley himself was ill.

"We are on the home stretch"—1872.

Shortly after losing the campaign, he also died. His supporters blamed Nast's cruel attacks.

Nast's final years were far from illustrious. In 1887 he left *Harper's Weekly* because of disagreements with the editor. Both the magazine and the cartoonist's career were seriously hurt by the move. Then an unfortunate investment caused Nast to lose most of his wealth. Struggling for a living, he accepted a position as a consul in Ecuador. There he died of malaria in 1902.

Thomas Nast is often called the "father of American political cartooning." His work helped give political cartoons an important place in American journalism. He opened the door for a host of cartoonists to follow. In spite of his shortcomings, Thomas Nast was a giant in his field.

Joseph Keppler
(1838-1894)

In the mid-19th century an Austrian boy named Joseph Keppler began to display artistic talent. He helped his father, a baker, decorate cakes. This was only the beginning. Joseph Keppler was to build a successful career on his creativity and imagination.

Keppler's career as a cartoonist began while he was still a young man. Even before he had finished his schooling at the Vienna Academy of Fine Arts, his humorous drawings were being published. But Keppler did not want a career in art. He preferred to think of himself as an actor, a comedian, and even an opera singer.

DISCARDED
COLUMBUS JUNIOR HIGH SCHOOL LIBRARY
LOS ANGELES CITY SCHOOLS

The cover for the first English edition of Keppler's *Puck* in 1877. The mischievous child stepping out of the eggshell is Puck, the magazine's masthead figure.

Joseph Keppler lived in Europe until he was 29. Then in 1867 he moved to St. Louis, Missouri. For a short time he worked as an actor. He also spent some time studying medicine. Finally, he turned to publishing. The result was *Puck*, a magazine written in the German language. In some ways *Puck* was successful. It was respected by its readers. More important, it helped establish Keppler's reputation as an artist with a talent for satire. Financially, however, it failed.

After his magazine's short life was over, Keppler moved to New York City. There he joined the art staff of *Frank Leslie's Illustrated Newspaper*. After a few years with *Leslie's* he was ready to revive *Puck*. This time it was a success. By 1877 Keppler was publishing an English edition of the magazine.

The English-language *Puck* became an important magazine in the late 1800s. For several years Keppler himself drew all the cartoons. He also drew a large cartoon for the cover and many of the ads for each week's edition. Parts of the magazine, which was the size of the modern *Life*, he did in color.

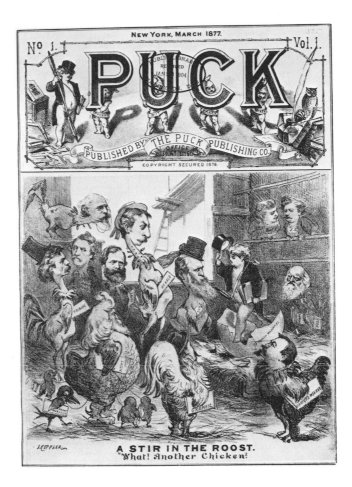

A STIR IN THE ROOST.
"What! Another Chicken!"

Joseph Keppler never achieved the great fame of his fellow cartoonist, Thomas Nast. Yet, in some ways, Nast could have learned from the *Puck* editor. For Keppler knew how to keep his work witty and gay. Still, he was capable of sharply criticizing many aspects of American society and politics.

During the 1880 presidential campaign, *Puck* printed one of Keppler's most daring cartoons. Entitled "Forbidding the Banns," the cartoon showed presidential candidate James A. Garfield as a bride. The bride's "wedding" to Uncle Sam was being interrupted by the discovery of an illegitimate child—a financial scandal. The American public was accustomed to seeing a political candidate accused of a shady financial deal. But to see him compared to an unwed mother was comic—and shocking.

"Forbidding the Banns"—1880.

"Bosses in the Senate"—1889. Keppler attacked the giant business trusts—the "moneybags"—that tried to control the United States Senate.

In keeping with his playful satire, Joseph Keppler pioneered in using caricature in his cartoons. His rival, Thomas Nast, drew faces that photographically resembled his subjects'. Nast feared that otherwise his readers wouldn't recognize the men he was portraying. Keppler, however, exaggerated the features of his subjects. This "caricature" made Keppler's cartoon figures more imaginative and humorous, and it didn't hurt his readers' ability to identify the men who were portrayed.

When Joseph Keppler died in February of 1894, *Puck* was one of America's leading magazines. And it outlived its founder for more than 20 years—a fine tribute to the talented man from Austria.

Frederick Burr Opper and his cartoon character Happy Hooligan.

Frederick Burr Opper

(1857-1937)

Political cartoonists do not agree on the importance of humor in their work. Some say that a political cartoonist seldom needs to make his audience laugh. Others argue that he must remain witty to help his reader "swallow the medicine." Frederick Burr Opper sided with the second group. His cartoons were first and foremost funny.

Opper was born in 1857 in the town of Madison, Ohio. He left school to seek his fortune when he was 14. Before he made his start as a cartoonist, he worked for a newspaper and a New York store. Then Opper began his career where other famous cartoonists had—*Frank Leslie's Illustrated*

Newspaper. After three years he went to work on Keppler's *Puck,* where he remained until 1899. Then, switching to the *New York Journal,* Opper spent the rest of his career with the Hearst newspaper syndicate.

Throughout his life, Opper was a versatile cartoonist. He was responsible for several comic strips and created such characters as Happy Hooligan. He illustrated humorous books by such authors as Mark Twain. And he commented on world affairs and happenings in the United States in his political cartoons.

Opper's light touch followed him into every assignment. In the 1890s large, powerful nations were "colonizing" poorer countries in Asia and Africa. Opper stood back and laughed at the greedy nations. In a cartoon for *Puck,* he showed England, France, Germany, Japan, and Russia all impressed with their own power and ready for a fight. Then he reminded Americans that they were no different. In the center he drew Uncle Sam with his sleeves rolled up and his fists clenched. "By gosh!" Uncle Sam exclaims. "I kin lick all creation."

Cartoon for the letter E in the series
"An Alphabet of Joyous Trusts"—1902.

Perhaps under the influence of the comic strip, Opper liked to create series of political cartoons, repeating a theme day after day. Two of these famous series were "The McKinley Minstrels" and "Alice in Plunderland." In one series, "An Alphabet of Joyous Trusts," he did his part in trying to help break the trusts—giant monopolies that gripped American business. When the series ended, he wrote:

> With these alphabet pictures the artist took pains
> But he's got to stop now, and with grief nearly busts
> 'Cause our language but twenty-six letters contains,
> Though our country contains twenty-six hundred Trusts.

33

Frederick Opper left the *New York Tribune* in 1932. Poor eyesight forced the cartoonist into retirement. But Opper's humor had not failed him. "I could no longer see the point of my cartoons," he joked. Five years later in New Rochelle, New York, Frederick Burr Opper died.

Homer Davenport
(1867-1912)

Frederick Burr Opper was careful to keep his political cartoons on the lighter side. One of his fellow cartoonists was more like Thomas Nast—not so kind to those he portrayed. This was Homer Davenport, a boy from the country who became New York City's highest paid political cartoonist. Davenport's pictures, it has been said, "invited battle and tears."

Homer Davenport was born in Silvertown, Oregon, in 1867. After holding several different jobs, he began newspaper work with the *Portland Oregonian*. Just three years later, Davenport found himself with the *New York Evening Journal*, where he became one of the nation's leading cartoonists.

Like other cartoonists of the times, Homer Davenport struck out at the practices of big business. His special target was Mark Hanna, an industrialist from Cleveland, Ohio. By 1892 Hanna was capably handling William McKinley's campaign for President. Hanna was especially capable at collecting funds from large corporations. Hanna and other big businessmen wanted assurance that the next President would believe as they did—that the government existed primarily to aid business. McKinley provided that assurance.

Historians tell us that Mark Hanna was an honest man in his own way. However, those who opposed him, including Davenport, saw him as a tyrant whose only goal was money. They feared that the government of the people would be forever lost to ruthless wealthy men.

"I am Confident the Workingmen are with Us."—1896. Davenport's cartoon of Mark Hanna uses the industrialist's own words as a caption.

McKinley won the election with Hanna's support. But Davenport's pencil had made the Republican boss look like the worst sort of villain. Hanna once showed a cartoon of Davenport's to a Senator. "That hurts," Hanna reportedly said, " . . . to be held up to the gaze of the world as a murderer of women and children. I tell you it hurts." Hanna walked away with tears rolling down his cheeks.

In 1904 Homer Davenport became an ardent Republican supporter of Teddy Roosevelt. In fact, the Republicans hired him to cartoon for Roosevelt. (It is reported that he had trouble collecting his pay.) For the man who was building a reputation as a "trust buster," Davenport drew his

"He's Good Enough for Me"—1904.

most famous cartoon. "He's Good Enough for Me" showed Uncle Sam standing approvingly behind Roosevelt. The cartoon was not humorous, but was a very effective campaign piece.

Davenport's cartoons made him famous and wealthy within a relatively short time. But the career of the Oregon cartoonist was not long-lasting. On May 2, 1912, Homer Davenport died, only 45 years of age.

William Glackens

(1870-1938)

"I cannot think of a happier life than the one my father lived. . . . He had known the best that life has to offer: a peaceful nature, a devoted wife, a happy home, delightful friends, and the contentment that comes from creative work untroubled by anyone's opinion, and he did not leave an enemy, for he had never had one." This describes the life of an outstanding American cartoonist, illustrator, and painter —William James Glackens. And it was the observation of someone who knew—his son, Ira.

William Glackens was born in Philadelphia in 1870. Although his life was contented and happy, it was not without adventure. After high school Glackens set out on trips most boys only talk about: a journey to Florida in a railroad boxcar, a boating expedition on the Delaware River, a year and a half in Paris.

Before his trip to Paris Glackens had already begun an art career with several Philadelphia newspapers. After his trip he returned to New York City and found a job with the *New York World*. Soon he switched to another newspaper, the *New York Herald*. He spent his spare time painting with a group of young artists, later called the "Ashcan School." Like others in the group, Glackens at that time chose to paint the dark, dreary scenes of the city.

Glackens spent his years with the newspapers during the "golden age" of cartooning and illustrating. Newspapers depended heavily on artists and cartoonists. Glackens was versatile. He contributed light, humorous sketches that won the praise of many critics. He also reported fires, parades, and other events. For example, Glackens and artist Harry Dart made two huge drawings for the *New York Herald* covering the inauguration parade of President William McKinley.

A sketch of President William McKinley's inauguration parade done by Glackens for *The New York Herald* in 1897.

Glackens had a rare gift for remembering detail. Seldom did he sketch at an event. Instead, he had trained himself to memorize a scene. Then he hurried back to his office where he reproduced it down to the last detail. (The McKinley parade drawings showed more than 40 horses, hundreds of marching soldiers, and even individuals in the crowd.)

Artist Everett Shinn claimed that Glackens could observe a fire engine passing in the street and then draw it so exactly that another engine could be built from his drawing.

During the Spanish-American War William Glackens was sent to Cuba by *McClure's* magazine. Like Thomas Nast during the Civil War, Glackens sent home drawings of the war action. These drawings are considered to be some of his best work.

"The Night After San Juan"—*McClure's*, 1898.

"Christmas Shoppers," Madison Square, New York City—about 1912.

However, the Spanish-American War ended Glackens' work as a recorder and interpreter of news. For a time he did magazine illustrations. But Glackens disliked illustrating. So he turned to painting—what he enjoyed most and for which he is best remembered. However, William Glackens of the "Ashcan School" had changed. There were no more dreary cityscapes. Instead he preferred to paint colorful portraits and gay park and cafe scenes. Today his paintings hang with the works of outstanding American artists.

Until he died at the age of 68 in Westport, Connecticut, William James Glackens' life was indeed ideal.

Self-portrait of Rollin Kirby

Rollin Kirby

(1875-1952)

In 1922 the first Pulitzer Prize for editorial cartooning was presented. One of the requirements for the prize was that the cartoon help some cause important to mankind. Five million of the Russian people recently had died from starvation. More were dying. The winning cartoon, "On the Road to Moscow," drew attention to this serious problem. The cartoonist was Rollin Kirby of the *New York World.* Before his career ended, Kirby was to win three of the coveted awards.

"On the Road to Moscow"—1922.

Kirby was born in Galva, Illinois, in 1875. After attending schools in Nebraska, he studied art in New York City and Paris. When his studies ended he began a career as a painter. But Kirby soon found that painting earned him very little money. He turned to illustrating for *Collier's*, *McClure's*, *Life*, and others. Then, in 1911 Kirby's career as a political cartoonist began with the *New York World*.

"Now, Then, All Together: 'My Country, 'Tis of Thee!'"—1920.
Rollin Kirby's Mr. Dry leads the nation in a patriotic song
during the gloomy days of Prohibition.

During the 1920s, one of Rollin Kirby's (and other
cartoonists') favorite targets was Prohibition. Kirby created
the grim "Mr. Dry," a famous cartoon figure that became a
common symbol for the Prohibition era. (When Prohibition
ended in 1933, the artist formally buried Mr. Dry in a
cartoon.)

"News of the Outside World"—1925.

Another favorite subject won Kirby his second Pulitzer Prize. Kirby's political views were liberal. He again and again strongly protested the failure of the United States to join the League of Nations, a world peace organization formed after World War I. In a cartoon entitled "The Accuser," he showed a Roman statesman (the United States Senate) standing with a sword over a dead body (Treaty of

Peace). A woman labeled "Humanity" points an accusing finger at the murderer. Kirby's prize-winning cartoon, "News of the Outside World," showed a hobo camp. The three hobos in the camp were the nations who had refused to join the League—the United States, Mexico, and Russia.

Rollin Kirby won his third Pulitzer Prize for "Tammany." Published in September 1928, the cartoon spread over seven columns of the *New York World*. For years the Democrats had been attacked for the corruption of their "Tammany Hall" in New York City. In his prize cartoon Kirby struck back at the Republicans. Reminding readers that corruption was not limited to the Democrats alone, the cartoonist caricatured the Republicans with their smug, holier-than-thou attitude. The cartoon aroused comments of every kind from all over. The paper later reported that "Tammany" stirred up more controversy than any other cartoon it had printed.

After 19 years Kirby left the *New York World*. He then worked for the *World Telegram, Saturday Evening Post,* and *Look*. He also tried his hand in another creative field— writing. He published some short plays, articles, and poems before his death in 1952.

Jay N. Darling

(1876-1962)

Near the turn of the century an angry faculty studied a signature at the bottom of a cartoon. The cartoon, drawn in a school yearbook, showed them as chorus girls. The signature read "Ding." Soon the mystery cartoonist was discovered. "Ding" was short for Darling—Jay Norwood Darling. Ding was suspended.

Jay Darling was born in Norwood, Michigan, the son of a minister. His school days were spent in Indiana and Iowa. He attended college in Beloit, Wisconsin. Ding started his career as a newspaper reporter for the *Sioux City Journal*. Soon he began to make sketches to accompany his stories. In 1900 his first political cartoon appeared in the *Journal*. That was the beginning of half a century of cartooning for Jay Darling.

"Why Call Them Sportsmen?"—1938.

While on his honeymoon in 1906, Ding was offered a job as an editorial cartoonist for the *Des Moines Register*. He accepted. After that, although Darling traveled widely, he made his home in Des Moines, Iowa.

Ding used his pencil to promote conservation, his favorite cause. Whenever possible he worked to save natural resources and wildlife. He was particularly worried about the future of wild ducks. In cartoons such as "Why Call Them Sportsmen?" he attacked game violators. This cartoon shows a battered, bandaged duck looking into a dictionary and saying, "Either this dictionary is wrong or there are a lot of folks around here calling themselves by the wrong name!"

"The Long, Long Trail"—1919.

As years went by, Ding's work for conservation brought him many awards and honors. He became founder and first president of the National Wildlife Federation. He received the Teddy Roosevelt Gold Medal Award. In 1933 his drawing of a wild duck appeared on the first federal duck stamp.

Ding was a friend to several Presidents. One of his most famous cartoons was drawn as a tribute to his friend Teddy Roosevelt, the "Rough Rider." "The Long, Long Trail" showed the nation in mourning for its former President. Herbert Hoover and the cartoonist were fishing companions. As a special favor to Hoover, Ding marked an "X" behind his name whenever he signed a cartoon. This ended the President's confusion as to who had really drawn the cartoon—Ding or his understudy, Tom Carlisle.

AN ORPHAN AT 8 IS NOW ONE OF THE WORLD'S GREATEST MINING ENGINEERS AND ECONOMISTS WHOSE AMBITION IS TO ELIMINATE THE CYCLE OF DEPRESSION AND UNEMPLOYMENT

THE SON OF A PLASTERER IS NOW THE WORLD'S GREATEST NEUROLOGIST AND HIS HOBBY IS GOOD HEALTH FOR POOR CHILDREN

A PRINTER'S APPRENTICE IS NOW CHIEF EXECUTIVE OF THE UNITED STATES

BUT THEY DIDN'T GET THERE BY HANGING AROUND THE CORNER DRUG STORE

"In Good Old U.S.A."—1923.

Twice Ding won the Pulitzer Prize for political cartooning. In 1923 he sketched the American ideal—poor boys making good. The cartoon, "In Good Old U.S.A.," had several parts, each showing a boy's rise to importance. The final section noted, "But they didn't get there by hanging around the corner drugstore."

"What a Place For a Waste Paper Salvage"—1943.

In 1943, when the Allies were fighting World War II, his prize winner was aimed at the unnecessary reports in government work. "What a Place For a Waste Paper Salvage" showed a mountain of reports, in triplicate, burying the nation's Capitol.

Darling's long career produced a mountain of cartoons (17,000), nationwide popularity, and a very substantial income. In 1949 Ding Darling retired, except for a few special assignments. And he lived to enjoy his retirement for over a decade.

Self-portrait of
Daniel Fitzpatrick

Daniel R. Fitzpatrick

(1891-1969)

Cartoon styles began to change in the 1920s and 1930s. Political cartoonists were moving away from busy drawings and labels to a more simple, direct style. One of the leaders of this change was Daniel R. Fitzpatrick of the *St. Louis Post-Dispatch*.

Fitzpatrick was born in Superior, Wisconsin, in 1891. After high school he attended the Chicago Art Institute. Fitzpatrick's career as a cartoonist began at the age of 20 with the *Chicago Daily News*. Shortly after, he moved to St. Louis, where he remained throughout his career with the *Post-Dispatch*.

Simple but powerful themes marked much of Fitz-patrick's work. In his cartoon "The Laws of Moses and the Laws of Today" he showed the simple tablets of Moses contrasted with the gigantic pile of laws of the modern world. Making his idea bold and clear paid off. Fitzpatrick won the Pulitzer Prize for his comparison in 1926.

"The Laws of Moses and the Laws of Today"—1925.

"Next!"—1939. A menacing machine shaped like
the Nazi swastika stands ready to roll over Poland.

More than earlier cartoonists, Fitzpatrick used symbols
to make his work dramatic. He drew fists, swords, globes,
and other symbols to show his reader an idea and make him
feel emotion. Instead of using clear, crisp lines, he often used
the side of his pencil or crayon. The soft edges and heavily
shaded areas added to the drama. It was this technique that
Fitzpatrick used in the 1930s to transform the Nazi swastika into a menacing symbol. Fitzpatrick's swastika came to
represent for Americans the evil of the Nazi movement.

"Journey's End"—1945.

One of his famous cartoons, "Journey's End," was drawn when Japan surrendered in World War II. Instead of showing a gay victory scene, Fitzpatrick reminded his readers of deeper, more serious meanings. On top of a burned globe, a few soldiers were shown pushing a flag marked "Victory" into a pile of rubble.

Fitzpatrick used the globe dramatically again when India and Pakistan were divided and torn by bloody strife. Sadly, Abraham Lincoln and Mohandas Gandhi look down on the world, disturbed by the trouble in the two countries. (The two leaders were often compared at that time by political cartoonists, as well as journalists, historians, and others. Both were great leaders at a time when their countries were torn by war. Both were assassinated.)

Daniel Fitzpatrick won many awards during his long career with the *Post-Dispatch*. Among these was a second Pulitzer Prize in 1955. He was also presented an honorary doctor of letters degree by Washington University in St. Louis. In a book of Fitzpatrick's cartoons, editor Ralph Coghlan wrote: "Sometimes these pictures burn with wit or irony; others have a terrific emotional thrust; and still others hold a civilized balance against foolish extremism."

Fitzpatrick's work has helped make it clear that a political cartoonist is not mainly a humorist. Nor is he mainly an artist. Instead, he must be a person with combined talent, wit, and insight. As Rollin Kirby once said, "A good cartoon consists of 75% idea and 25% drawing."

William Gropper

(1897-   )

Nearly every political cartoonist has his favorite subject. Thomas Nast attacked Tammany Hall many times, while Ding Darling helped the cause of conservation whenever possible. William Gropper's favorite subject was one capable of stirring up more emotion and disagreement than Ding's ducks or even Nast's "Boss" Tweed. Many of Gropper's cartoons criticized the workings of the capitalist system. Some who do not share Gropper's attitudes have called his cartoons propaganda.

William Gropper was born in New York City in 1897. As a child he lived in extreme poverty. He managed to win a scholarship, however, and was able to study at the National Academy of Design and the New York School of Fine and Applied Art. In 1919 Gropper launched his career as a newspaper artist with the *New York Herald Tribune*. But Gropper became disturbed by the paper's business practices and left the *Tribune* in the same year. He later became a staff cartoonist for the *New York Post* and for the *Morning Freiheit*, a Communist paper. (Gropper was not a member of the Communist Party, but he did sympathize with some of its ideas for improving society.)

Perhaps the poverty Gropper knew as a child made him very sensitive to social wrongs. At any rate, Gropper believed that "the artist should be at all times progressive in his ideas and fight against reactionary groups." So, using a style even stronger than Fitzpatrick's, he struck out in his cartoons at what he saw as the wrongs in American society.

Some of Gropper's cartoons, such as "Business," may not seem so shocking now. Others, such as "The Law," might have been drawn yesterday because there is still violent disagreement on the issue the cartoonist attacked.

"Business"—about 1935.

"The Law"—about 1935.

The artist did not limit his criticism to politics within the United States. He distrusted powerful leaders everywhere. For example, he struck out many times at Japan's Emperor Hirohito. In 1936 Gropper was aware of Japan's aggressive policies and saw war on the horizon. He drew the Emperor hauling the Nobel Peace Prize away in a cart.

"Another Pact"—1936.

One of his famous cartoons, "Another Pact," was drawn when Hitler and Mussolini formed the Rome-Berlin Axis. While many people refused to take the two leaders seriously, Gropper feared another war. He drew Mussolini and Hitler standing on top of a skull, shaking hands.

William Gropper published several books, including *The Golden Land* and *Lidice*. After a trip to Russia he created *Drawings of the U.S.S.R.* Gropper was also a notable painter who expressed his views in paintings such as "The Senate," "The Opposition," and "Minorities." William Gropper's work as an artist and cartoonist—the work of one of America's radical spokesmen—is considered by many critics to be of the highest quality.

Herbert L. Block

(1909-   )

One of the best known signatures in the corner of political cartoons today is "Herblock"—Herbert L. Block of the *Washington Post*. Herblock has been called a master of political cartoonists, a man of rare skill whose sketches portray the wit and irony of a situation and not merely his own views.

Herblock has been known for taking strong stands on issues before other cartoonists are willing to tangle with them. Even before World War II broke out Herblock had the foresight to attack Hitler while others did not yet fear the German leader. After World War II Herblock was one of the few men brave enough to attack Senator Joe McCarthy.

"I Have Here In My Hand—"—1954. A Herblock cartoon of Senator Joe McCarthy.

McCarthy had grabbed publicity and terrified the nation with his insistence that Communists controlled the United States. Loyal Americans convinced by McCarthy's evidence set out to rid the country of Communists, in what resembled a mad "witch hunt." One of Herblock's most damning cartoons showed McCarthy making a speech, holding in one hand a "faked letter" and in the other a "doctored photo."

Herbert Block was born in Chicago in 1909. Although his father was a chemist, Herblock chose art as his field and won a scholarship to the Chicago Art Institute. But he did not finish his art training. In 1920 he took a job as a cartoonist for the *Chicago Daily News*. Later he joined the Newspaper Enterprise Association in Cleveland, Ohio. From there the name of "Herblock" became familiar to readers throughout the nation. After World War II Herblock joined the *Washington Post*.

Politically independent, Herblock has delighted in taking pokes at both Republicans and Democrats. However, in general the cartoonist aims his fire at individuals rather than political parties. One of Herblock's favorite targets for many years has been Richard Nixon.

During his career, Herblock has won many awards, including two Pulitzer Prizes. His 1942 prize-winning cartoon was titled "British Plane." In it a scowling German soldier searches the sky as a plane goes over. Two Parisians watch his gaze and smile secretly. Herblock's 1954 prize winner was prompted by Stalin's death. The cartoon shows Death saying to the Russian tyrant, "You were always a great friend of mine, Joseph." Herblock has also published several books of his cartoons, such as *Herblock's Here and Now* and *Straight Herblock*.

"British Plane"—1942.

"You Were Always A Great Friend Of Mine, Joseph"— 1953.

According to Herblock, good political cartoons are not the result of inspiration. "The work," he says, "is like that of a columnist or editorial writer—to find out as much as you can and then to put it down on paper." Nor does he believe there are specific rules for the cartoonist. "I don't think an editorial cartoon necessarily has to be funny —with or without words. The only rules are general rules—it should be simple, and you should say something."

Herblock has said a great deal through his cartoons, and continues to do so. His name will go down among America's greatest cartoonists.

Bill Mauldin

(1921-   )

John F. Kennedy had been assassinated. Bill Mauldin, political cartoonist for the *Chicago Sun-Times*, had to come up with a cartoon for a nation jolted by tragedy. Later, in his book *I've Decided I Want My Seat Back*, he wrote:

> What to draw? Grief, sorrow, tears weren't enough for this event. There had to be monumental shock. Monument . . . shock . . . a cartoon idea is nothing more or less than free association. What is more shocking than a statue come alive, showing emotion? Assassination. Civil rights. There was only one statue for this.

At 2:15 Mauldin started to draw his cartoon. By 3:00 P.M. he had finished. At 4:45, November 22, 1963, the first edition of the *Chicago Sun-Times* came off the press.

Mauldin's cartoon for the *Chicago Sun-Times* the day President John F. Kennedy was assassinated—November 22, 1963.

Mauldin's cartoon was in it. In his marble seat Abraham Lincoln had come alive, bent in grief, his head in his hands. Of all the words spoken in the days after Kennedy's death, none matched the eloquence of Bill Mauldin's cartoon.

"Go ahead, Joe. If ya don't bust it ya'll worry about it all night"—1944. One of Mauldin's famous "Willie and Joe" cartoons.

Bill Mauldin's career as a cartoonist began in the Army during World War II. A young man from Arizona, Bill had had some art training at the Chicago Art Institute. In the Army he was put to work covering battle campaigns and drawing cartoons for a divisional newspaper. Reports about the war that were sent back home bothered Mauldin. Frequently stories were changed before they were printed in the United States. He decided to show the American people what the war was really like. The result was the "Willie and Joe" cartoon series. Its main characters were two soldiers who lived from day to day as best they could—quite unlike the soldiers in glamorous news reports. The "Willie and Joe" cartoons and stories were collected in a book, *Up Front*, which became a best seller. For services beyond the call of duty, Mauldin earned the Purple Heart, the Legion of Merit —and the Pulitzer Prize. At 23 he was the youngest person ever to receive the award.

Mauldin returned from the war with a great career ahead of him. He began work with the United Feature Syndicate. Later, he covered the Korean War for *Collier's* magazine. In 1958 he joined the *St. Louis Post-Dispatch*. There he earned his second Pulitzer Prize. The prize cartoon depicted prisoners in a Siberian Labor Camp, guarded by a Russian soldier. "I won the Nobel Prize for literature," one prisoner tells the other. "What was your crime?" In 1962 Mauldin went to the *Chicago Sun-Times*.

"I Won the Nobel Prize for Literature. What was your Crime?"—1958.

"You ain't gaining much altitude holding me down"—1962.

Mauldin has said that cartoonists shouldn't try to mold public opinion. He feels their job is to bring subjects to a reader's attention. After that "it really doesn't matter whether we needle him, amuse him, or infuriate him. We've got his mind on the matter—and what he does about it next is his own business." However, during the 1960s Mauldin did his part to influence public opinion on the Civil Rights movement. The cartoonist especially devoted his talent to making those Southern "rednecks" who opposed Negro rights look ridiculous.

Today, as the *New York Times* has noted, Bill Mauldin "is at the top of his field—a lonely plateau reached by no other contemporary cartoonist."

Bill Sanders

(1932-   )

In addition to Herblock and Mauldin, there are a dozen or more outstanding young cartoonists working today. One of them is Bill Sanders, whose work appears in newspapers throughout the country. Like Herblock, Sanders is known for the sharpness of his bite and his tendency to attack courageously wherever an attack seems needed. But Bill's cartoons are usually humorous as well as pointed.

Born in Tennessee and raised in Florida, William Willard "Bill" Sanders' interest in art supposedly began when his sixth-grade teacher asked him to draw "a fox jumping over a log." Bill did the drawing and his teacher praised it so much that Sanders began to think he had artistic talent. But during high school, Bill was more interested in football than in art. And football was interested in Bill.

"That's funny . . . my government keeps telling me it's a peace symbol, too"—1971. Sanders takes a poke at the idea promoted by governments that nuclear weapons help to keep the peace.

He won a football scholarship to Western Kentucky University, and in 1953 set the National Collegiate Athletic Association's record for pass completions: 66.8 percent. Then in 1954 he was asked to sign a professional tryout contract with the Cleveland Browns. But Bill graduated from college with a degree in English literature, got married, and left for the Korean War instead.

Six months after Sanders had been assigned to head a mortar platoon, he decided it was time to begin a career in art. With luck and a little fast talking, Sanders was able to land a job running the *Stars and Stripes* printing plant in Seoul, Korea. In 1957, when the Russians launched Sputnik, Sanders penned his first published cartoon. It showed a lazy Uncle Sam "in the doghouse" while Sputnik whizzed by over his head. In 1959 Bill returned to the States, where he was offered a job as editorial cartoonist with the *Greensboro North Carolina Daily News*. After that, fame came quickly to Bill Sanders. In 1963 he moved to the *Kansas City Star*, and in 1967 to *The Milwaukee Journal*. The Association of American Editorial Cartoonists elected him their president for 1966-67.

Throughout his career, Bill Sanders has fought for editorial freedom for cartoonists. One of his most famous cartoons, "Snow White and Her Million Dwarfs," shows why such freedom is necessary. The cartoon features an ape-mother who has produced millions of unwanted children. Sanders uses the ape-mother as a symbol for laws against abortion and birth control. Although she is stupid looking and ugly, the ape-mother is called "Snow White"— a name that makes us think of a kind, beautiful princess.

THE MILWAUKEE JOURNAL

ARCHAIC ABORTION AND BIRTH CONTROL LAWS

UNWANTED, UNLOVED & UNDERNOURISHED CHILDREN

"Snow White and Her Million Dwarfs"—1970.

The cartoon illustrates Sanders' belief that anti-abortion and anti-birth control laws are stupid and bad. In his opinion they encourage the creation of millions of unwanted and neglected children. Saying that they are wise and good doesn't make them so—anymore than calling the ape-mother Snow White makes her a beautiful princess. A newspaper worried about offending its readers might never allow a cartoonist who did not have editorial freedom to see a work like this in print—as Bill Sanders well knows.

Ray Osrin

(1928-   )

Raymond Harold Osrin, editorial cartoonist for the *Cleveland Plain Dealer*, is a native of Brooklyn, New York. Ray has jokingly claimed that being dropped on his head when he was two years old gave him the inspiration to be a cartoonist. Joking aside, Osrin's interest in cartooning does seem to have developed early. Ray went to work in 1945 for a publisher of comic books, even before he had graduated from high school. For the next 12 years, he turned out work for hundreds of comic books. During the same period of time, he also finished high school, married, began a family, and attended the Art Students League of New York.

"The Thinker"—1970. Osrin's takeoff on a famous statue warns man to act to save his environment before it's too late.

In 1957 the cartoonist moved from New York to Pittsburgh, Pennsylvania. There he did animated illustrations for television and also illustrations for the *Pittsburgh Press*. In 1963 Ray Osrin joined the staff of the *Plain Dealer*, and a few years later he was selected to replace that newspaper's retiring cartoonist, Ed Keukes. Since that appointment, Osrin has been singled out many times for awards for outstanding cartooning. His cartoons are reprinted in major newspapers and newsmagazines throughout the country.

"The Best Watchdog"—1971. Osrin points out the importance of a free press.

Most of Osrin's cartoons point up the day's issues with a touch of humor. But Osrin's pen is also capable of turning out biting, serious criticism. Like his fellow cartoonists, he is very concerned with the problem of editorial freedom. He has said that he feels "the cartoonist's main battle is always with his own paper in fighting for the degree of freedom he needs to work best." For Osrin that means the freedom to take pokes or stabs at follies he sees wherever he sees them. Ray Osrin refuses to be identified with any one political camp or any one set of social principles.

Wayne Stayskal

(1931-   )

Wayne Stayskal of *Chicago Today* is a highly respected editorial cartoonist whose sense of humor never fails him. Most of his cartoons are editorials on modern life rather than stabs at particular individuals or political situations. Stayskal has a light touch; he rarely attacks an enemy head-on. In fact, his approach to cartooning resembles Frederick Burr Opper's. Opper would have approved of the advice Wayne once gave a young man hoping to become a cartoonist: "Don't berate anybody or anything without making sure you are on very solid ground. Poke funny—try not to be mean."

Stayskal is a native of Chicago. After graduating from high school, he served four years in the U.S. Air Force. Then he returned to attend the Chicago Academy of Fine Arts. In 1957 Wayne Stayskal joined the staff of the *Chicago American* (now called *Chicago Today*) as a layout artist for the newspaper's Sunday magazine. At the time, Wayne had no intention of becoming an editorial cartoonist. But after he had been with the paper a few years, he asked to try his hand at doing a few cartoons on the local scene—in addition to working at his regular job.

"Chief . . . I Think We Finally Pinpointed the Bomber's Hideout"—1971. Police inefficiency is the target for one of Stayskal's humor-tipped arrows.

"Better! . . . Much Better! . . . Right, Reverend?"—1971.
Stayskal makes some of the controversy over film ratings
look like foolishness.

Wayne began by doing a cartoon once in awhile, but in short time he was being asked to create a few cartoons each month. Then Stayskal was given a big break. In 1962 when the well-known cartoonist Vaughn Shoemaker came to *Chicago Today*, Wayne was named his assistant. He did two cartoons a week under the master's guidance, and his talent was soon recognized. Today Stayskal is an independent and highly successful syndicated cartoonist who has been described as "a master lampooner of current events."

Tom Darcy

(1932-   )

Tom Darcy, editorial cartoonist with *Newsday* of Long Island, pens hard-hitting cartoons. Cleverness and insight coupled with the willingness to tackle controversial problems have brought Darcy the kind of recognition and following given few cartoonists. However, Darcy's determination to speak sharply and honestly through his cartoons has often made his life difficult.

Born in Brooklyn in 1932, Thomas Francis Darcy graduated from the School of Visual Arts in New York in 1957. He then joined the staff of *Newsday*, becoming, at the age of 24, the youngest editorial cartoonist in the nation.

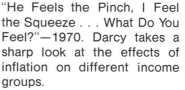

"He Feels the Pinch, I Feel the Squeeze . . . What Do You Feel?"—1970. Darcy takes a sharp look at the effects of inflation on different income groups.

Two years later, in 1959, Darcy left *Newsday* because he felt the newspaper did not offer him the freedom he needed as a cartoonist. But it was not easy for the young cartoonist to find a position with a liberal newspaper. Many papers tend to be moderate or conservative in their points of view and editorial policies. Tom searched without luck for five years, supporting himself and his family by taking odd jobs at everything from magazine sales to farm labor. Then Darcy tried working for three different conservative papers in a row—the *Phoenix Gazette*, the *Houston Post*, and the *Philadelphia Bulletin*. But not until 1968, when the cartoonist was brought back to *Newsday* by a new, liberal publisher, did Darcy find an editorial home. He then quickly settled down to do the kind of intense and honest cartooning he has become famous for.

In recent years, Tom Darcy has collected eight major awards for excellence in editorial cartooning, including the Pulitzer Prize in 1970. Always eager to handle the most controversial issues of the day, he has established himself as one of the leading political cartoonists in the United States.

"Monday's TV Listing: 'Romper Room,' 'Playschool,' 'Galloping Gourmet,' 'Laugh-In,' 'Bright Promise,' 'This Is Your Life'"—1970. Darcy attacks society for ignoring the existence of extreme poverty.

Cartoonists Today

One of the qualities modern cartoonists share is a deep sense of responsibility to the public. Most cartoonists believe their job is to draw people's attention to important issues. But many of them feel a cartoonist should not limit himself to looking at political problems and situations. He has the responsibility to present points of view on economic and social as well as political issues. Some cartoonists, like Wayne Stayskal, devote most of their attention to matters which are not strictly political. This is one reason why serious cartoonists today prefer to be called "editorial cartoonists." The name "political cartoonists" is becoming inappropriate.

Modern cartoonists also share a deep concern for the status of their profession. Together, they are demanding the same freedom of expression normally granted by newspapers to editorial writers. They base their argument in part on the fact that cartoons serve the same function as written editorials. And they actively point out that some of the best work in their field has been done by cartoonists working for newspapers which did permit freedom of expression. Herblock, for example, was free to support Adlai Stevenson when he ran for President of the United States in the 1950s, even though Herblock's newspaper, the *Washington Post*, was completely behind Dwight Eisenhower.

Earlier in this century there was some worry that cartooning was a dying art. Today, however, cartooning looks strong and healthy because of the outstanding work being done by a number of cartoonists. Unfortunately, only a few cartoonists could be included in this book. There are many others whose names deserve mention—Draper Hill, Ed Valtman, Paul Szep, Patrick Oliphant, Hugh Haynie, Jules Feiffer, and Paul Conrad, among others. The cartoons these men do are valuable, perhaps more so today than in the past, because they make people think about important issues from different points of view.

The Pull Ahead Books

AMERICA'S FIRST LADIES
  1789 to 1865

AMERICA'S FIRST LADIES
  1865 to the Present Day

DARING SEA CAPTAINS

DOERS AND DREAMERS

FAMOUS CHESS PLAYERS

FAMOUS CRIMEFIGHTERS

FAMOUS SPIES

GREAT AMERICAN NATURALISTS

INDIAN CHIEFS

PIRATES AND BUCCANEERS

POLITICAL CARTOONISTS

PRESIDENTIAL LOSERS

SINGERS OF THE BLUES

STARS OF THE ZIEGFELD FOLLIES

WESTERN LAWMEN

WESTERN OUTLAWS

We specialize in publishing quality books for young people. For a complete list please write

Lerner Publications Company

241 First Avenue North, Minneapolis, Minnesota 55401